D0359655

Werewolves

and Stories about Them

Eric Kudalis

Capstone Press

M I N N E A P O L I S

Printed in the United States of America.

Capstone Press • 2440 Fernbrook Lane • Minneapolis, MN 55447

Editorial Director   John Coughlan
Managing Editor   John Martin
Copy Editor   Theresa Early
Editorial Assistant   Michelle Wood

Library of Congress Cataloging-in-Publication Data

Kudalis, Eric, 1960-
    Werewolves and stories about them / Eric Kudalis.
        p. cm. -- (Classic monster stories)
    Includes bibliographical references and index.
    ISBN 1-56065-215-2 (lib. bdg.)
    1. Werewolves--Juvenile literature.   [1. Werewolves.]
I. Title. II. Series.
GR830.W4K83   1994
398.24'54--dc20   93-42830
                                                CIP
                                                 AC

Table of Contents

Chapter 1
The Wolf Man

Werewolf stories and **legends** have long been told wherever there are wolves. One of the best-known werewolf stories appears in the classic movie of 1941, *The Wolf Man*.

The Wolf Man

Larry Talbot drove toward his father's castle in Wales. This was the first time in 18 years that he had been home.

Larry's father, Sir John Talbot, greeted him at the door.

"It's good to have you back," Sir John said.

Meeting Gwen

Larry looked out through his father's telescope. The village came into view.

People below went about their business. Children dashed along the sidewalks. Cars passed on the streets.

Larry saw a beautiful woman in an antique shop.

That afternoon, Larry went to the shop. The woman stood behind the counter. Her name was Gwen Conliffe.

The Sign of the Werewolf

Larry wandered toward the walking sticks.

Gwen held up a cane with a silver cap. "This is a nice one."

"Look, it has a silver handle in the shape of a dog," Larry said.

"That's not a dog, it's a wolf," Gwen said. "The five-pointed star next to the wolf is a pentagram. It's the sign of a werewolf. Every werewolf is marked with it. So is his next victim. The silver will protect you from werewolf attacks."

She then recited a poem:

> *Even a man who is pure in heart*
> *And says his prayers at night*
> *May become a wolf when the **wolfsbane** blooms*
> *And the autumn moon is bright.*

Going to the Gypsy Festival

Larry did not believe in werewolves. They were only a **superstition**.

He decided to buy the cane anyway. As he was leaving the shop, a group of Gypsies came by.

"They are here for the festival in the woods tonight," Gwen told him.

"Let's go together," Larry said.

Gwen hesitated. She smiled without saying yes or no.

That night, Larry met Gwen.

"Jenny is coming with us," she said.

Jenny Williams was Gwen's friend. Gwen liked Larry, but she wasn't about to go to the festival alone with him.

They walked through the woods. As the moon shone through the branches, Jenny saw wolfsbane in full bloom.

Jenny picked the wolfsbane and recited the poem that Gwen had told Larry.

The Fortune-Teller

At the Gypsy camp, an old woman greeted them. Her name was Maleva.

"You've come to have your fortune read?" she asked. They nodded.

Jenny asked to go first. Maleva led her into a tent, where her son Bela sat at a small table.

Bela took Jenny's hands and looked at her palms. His expression grew tense. The full moon was rising. In Jenny's palm was the sign of the werewolf.

Jenny sensed something was wrong.

"What is it?" she asked.

"I can tell you nothing," Bela said. "Leave now before it's too late."

The Wolf Attack

Larry and Gwen saw Jenny dash into the dark woods. Jenny screamed. In a panic, Larry ran toward the scream.

A wolf was attacking Jenny. It sank its teeth into her neck.

The wolf man waits in the dark woods.

Larry threw the wolf aside, but it ripped at his clothes. He felt the fangs dig into his chest.

Larry grabbed his silver-capped cane. With four firm smacks, he cracked the wolf's skull.

Gwen ran to Larry as he lay bleeding. Maleva, the Gypsy woman, rode up on her horse-drawn cart.

When she saw the dead wolf, she was afraid. She saw the gashes in Larry's chest.

"The wolf bit you. May God help you now."

"There Was No Wolf."

When Larry got home, he told his father about the wolf attack. Captain Paul Montford went to investigate.

He found Jenny's lifeless body. Bela the Gypsy lay dead nearby. His skull was crushed.

"We found this silver cane next to Bela's body," Montford told Larry the next morning. "Do you know anything about it?"

"That's my cane. I used it to kill the wolf," he said.

"There was no wolf," Montford said.

"Of course there was a wolf. He bit me on the chest. See! Here are the fang marks."

Larry pulled open his shirt, but there were no marks.

"That's odd. How could I heal overnight?"

"It was dark and you were in a panic," Sir John Talbot said. "The wolf tore at your clothes but did not bite you. You thought Bela was the wolf. His death was an accident."

Sir John insisted that his son get some rest.

"Whoever Is Bitten Becomes a Werewolf"

That night, Larry stumbled into Maleva's camp.

"I knew you would come," she said to Larry. "Bela was a werewolf. Now you are cursed. Whoever is bitten by a werewolf becomes a werewolf when the full moon rises."

"You're lying!" Larry cried. "Werewolves don't exist."

"Let me see your chest."

Whoever is bitten by a werewolf becomes a werewolf.

Larry opened his shirt. There was the pentagram. Maleva said, "You are now a werewolf yourself. May heaven help you."

14

Larry had to get away from Maleva. He felt strange and hot as he ran back to Castle Talbot. Something was itching at his neck and legs.

He ran up to his room and locked the door. His clothes felt tight. His shoes felt small.

Larry kicked off his shoes. Hair covered his feet. He pulled up his pant legs. Thick brown hair covered his legs. Hair sprouted between his fingers and up his wrists.

Now a Werewolf

Larry was losing control. He growled and barked and paced restlessly in his room. Then he leaped out an open window.

His hair was thick as a wolf's coat. Fangs grew. Larry stalked through the village.

With the moon as his guide, he made his way to the cemetery.

There he saw a grave digger. Larry sprang at the man. Growling, he sank his fangs into the grave digger's neck.

Satisfied, he stood on a boulder and howled at the moon. Larry was now a werewolf.

A Feeling of Guilt

The next morning, Larry woke suddenly. He had dirt between his fingers and a bitter taste in his mouth. He saw mud on the windowsill.

He felt that he was guilty of some crime, but he didn't know what. Larry couldn't remember anything from the night before.

Sir John knocked at the door. He came in with Captain Montford.

"There was another killing last night," Montford said. "The police found a grave digger in the cemetery. It looks as though a wolf attacked him."

Montford said the police would set traps in the woods that night.

When Montford left, Larry asked his father, "What's all this about werewolves?"

"Werewolves have always been part of legend in these rural villages," Sir John said. "But werewolves don't exist. There is a mental condition called *lycanthropy*, in which a man believes he can become a wolf."

Larry became restless. He kept seeing the grave digger struggling with some great beast. He could taste blood.

No Escape from Fate

Once again, Larry grew claws and thick hair and fangs. He barked at the moon and dashed through the woods.

As he hunted for his next victim, something snapped around his ankles. He fell to the ground. He was caught in a wolf trap.

Maleva came by. She kneeled over him and undid the trap. He was transformed back into a human.

Larry looked at Maleva and began to cry. He knew it was true. He was a werewolf. There was no escape from his horrible fate.

A Warning for Gwen

Larry had to warn Gwen. He went to the antique shop and told her that he was going away forever. He wanted to protect Gwen and the town from further harm.

Gwen was not scared. "This charm I wear around my neck will protect me from evil," she said.

When Gwen held out her hand to Larry, he saw the pentagram in her palm. He knew she would be his next victim.

"No, I can't let you. Please, stay away from me," he cried. He ran from the shop.

"I Will Kill Again"

Larry told his father that he was a werewolf.

"You're just upset about the recent killings," Sir John said. "You need rest."

"I will kill again if you don't help me," Larry said. "Tie me up in the tower and don't let me free until morning."

Sir John still didn't believe Larry was a werewolf. He tied Larry up anyway.

Before Sir John left, Larry said, "Take my cane with you. It will protect you if I escape."

The wolf man
surprises his
victim.

Sir John took the cane to quiet Larry down. He then left him alone.

As the moon passed over Castle Talbot, Larry felt a strange burning sensation. The ropes couldn't hold him. A werewolf once again, he fled into the night.

The Werewolf's End

The werewolf could hear the men and the barking dogs searching the woods. He saw Gwen running toward the castle.

He threw his head back and howled.

He sprang on Gwen. She thrashed and screamed.

Townspeople rushed from all directions to Gwen's rescue.

Sir John whirled the cane against the beast's head.

The wolf clawed at Sir John. Sir John smashed the cane downward again and again until the wolf was dead.

Sir John prepares to strike the wolf man with his cane.

The group was quiet. They formed a circle around the wolf. They stared as the wolf turned back into Larry.

Sir John fell backward. His son was a werewolf. He had killed his own son.

"Your Suffering is Over"

Maleva pushed through the group at the grave. She stood over Larry. She repeated what she had said over her own son's grave:

> "The way you walked was thorny, but it was no fault of yours. As the rain enters the soil, the river enters the sea, so tears run to a **predestined** end. Your suffering is over, my son. Now you will find peace for **eternity**."

The wolf man was dead.

Goya, a Spanish artist, often used monsters such as werewolves and vampires in his art.

Chapter 2

Werewolf Legends In History

People have told stories about werewolves for centuries. According to legend, werewolves were human beings who changed into wolves at night. They were stronger and faster than ordinary wolves and as smart as humans.

Once a werewolf ate its fill of blood and flesh, it turned back into a human. Some stories said that anyone bitten by a werewolf would also become a werewolf. Werewolves usually changed when the moon was full.

Ancient Werewolves

The first story of a wolf man comes from Greek **mythology**. The king Lycaeon tried to serve a dinner of human flesh to Zeus, the most powerful Greek god. To punish Lycaeon, Zeus turned him into a wolf.

According to the story, Lycaeon's clothes then changed into wolf's hair, and his arms became legs.

Werewolf Tales in Europe

In Europe during the Middle Ages (500 to 1,500 years ago), werewolf tales were told because of the threat of wolf attacks.

Throughout Europe there were vicious wolf attacks. Packs of wolves roamed the countryside in search of food.

If wolves could not find animals to eat, they sometimes attacked humans. This happened very rarely, but it scared people. Many people were afraid to travel alone for fear of wolves. Wolves were considered evil. Werewolf tales became common throughout Europe.

Zeus turns Lycaeon into a wolf.

A German Werewolf

One of the strangest werewolf cases happened near Cologne, Germany, in the late 1500s. A wolf was leaving arms, legs, heads, and bodies in the fields. The villagers were too frightened to leave their houses.

The authorities finally spotted the wolf and surrounded it. To their surprise, the wolf was a man named Peter Stubbe, wearing a wolf's hide.

Stubbe said that he changed into a werewolf by strapping on the skin of a wolf. Stubbe was insane. He eventually confessed to 16 murders, for which he was **executed**.

Werewolf attacking humans. From Johannes Geiler von Kaiserberg, Die Emeis, fol. XLI (1516).

Chapter 3

How to Explain Werewolves

In *The Wolf Man*, Sir John Talbot tells Larry about a mental condition called *lycanthropy*.

Lycanthropy, or werewolfism, is a mental disorder in which a person imagines he or she has turned into a wolf or a werewolf.

A Chemical Cause of Lycanthropy

Scientists have found a chemical that may explain why so many people in the Middle Ages suffered from lycanthropy. The chemical is found in a plant called belladonna.

Belladonna was used by doctors to treat headaches and other health problems. Too many doses, however, can cause **hallucinations**. People who are hallucinating imagine things as clearly as if they were real.

A Fungus in Grain

The food people ate during the Middle Ages also may have caused lycanthropy. A **fungus** often grew on the grain used for making bread. This fungus, called *ergot*, brought on hallucinations.

In 1951, more than 130 people were hospitalized for ergot poisoning in Pont St. Esprit, France. They had eaten bread made with infected rye. Some of the victims thought that they had turned into beasts.

Other Werewolf Explanations

Many werewolf cases may be explained by **mass hysteria**. When events happened that were hard to explain, people became frightened. Sometimes a whole town or community panicked.

Gruesome murders or wolf attacks led people to accuse others of being werewolves.

Those who were accused were often executed.

Chapter 4
Real Wolves

In most werewolf legends, wolves are bloodthirsty creatures who attack humans. In reality, wolves do not attack people. This is just one of many misunderstandings about wolves.

At one time, wolves roamed almost half the world. The only places wolves didn't live were deserts, tropical rain forests, and high mountain ranges. Today wolves live in very few areas of the world.

Wolf Behavior

Wolves are interesting animals. The more you understand about their **behavior**, the less fearsome they seem.

Scenes like this one often make people scared of wolves. The key to overcoming the fear of wolves is understanding their behavior.

Wolves are the direct **ancestors** of dogs. They live in highly organized groups called *packs*. About 20 wolves make up each pack. Each animal has its own rank in the pack. The alpha male is the leader. The alpha female is leader of the females.

An important part of wolf "language" is the howl. Wolves often howl together, before a hunt or just to show their togetherness. A wolf that is alone might howl by itself. This is the lonely cry that people associate with wolves.

Hardy Survivors

Wolves hunt for large animals such as moose and deer. They also eat small animals such as rabbits or mice.

Packs go for as long as two weeks without food. The head male and female always eat first. The other pack members take their turns in order of rank. The lowest-ranking wolf eats last.

Wolves live in organized groups called packs.

Usually only the alpha male and the alpha female mate. As many as seven pups will be born in a wolf litter. Every wolf in the pack helps raise the pups. They all bring food to the mother and pups.

In order to protect the wolf, scientists like David Mech study their habits. Here, Mech draws blood from a timberwolf.

Chapter 5

Wolves and People

In werewolf stories such as *The Wolf Man,* people fear wolves and try to kill them. This feeling was common until recently. Wolves have been hunted so much that in many places there are none left.

An Endangered Species
Wolves have been completely destroyed in most of Europe. Only a few wolves are left in northern Spain and Eastern Europe.

Canada and Alaska have about 20,000 to 25,000 wolves left. About 1,000 wolves live in Minnesota.

David Mech sits next to three illegally killed (or poached) wolves.

A few wolves can be spotted in Glacier National Park in Montana and the Upper Peninsula of Michigan.

Studying Wolves

Today many people study wolves rather than hunt them. They learn about the activities, movement, and **territory** of wolf packs.

One man who studies wolves is David Mech. He has tracked wolves in the woods of northern Minnesota by using **radio collars**. He learns about the habits, movement, and territory of wolf packs.

People are beginning to understand and respect the wolf.

Since wolves move over a large territory it is often necessary to study them from an airplane. Here David Mech looks down on a wolf pack in northern Minnesota.

Although Gypsies are traditionally known as fortune-tellers and entertainers, today they work in all occupations.

Chapter 6

Who Are the Gypsies?

In *The Wolf Man*, Larry Talbot visits a Gypsy fortune-teller. Gypsies are a group of **nomadic**, or wandering, people. They live in almost every part of the world. The largest number live in Eastern Europe.

The ancestors of the Gypsies were a people who came from India in the 1400s. They said they were from "Little Egypt." The word *Gypsy* comes from "Egypt."

Most Gypsies are part of the Rom tribe, and they refer to themselves as Rom. They have their own language, Romani, and their own dance, music, and food.

Gypsies were traditionally known as fortune-tellers, metal workers, horse traders, and entertainers, but today they hold every kind of job.

While the Roms are thought to move from place to place, most Gypsies, in fact, live in one place, much as non-Gypsies do.

Throughout history, Gypsies have faced **prejudice** and **persecution**. More than a million Gypsies, for example, were killed in the **Holocaust** of World War II.

Glossary

ancestor–a many-times-great grandparent

behavior–the way something acts and lives

eternity–all future time; ever after

executed–killed by the government as punishment

fungus–a simple plant such as a mold

hallucination–something seen or imagined so strongly that the person imagining it believes it is real

Holocaust–a program of the German government during World War II (1939-1945) to kill people, such as Jews, Gypsies, and mentally retarded people, who did not fit the model of an "ideal German"

legend–an old story

lycanthropy–the belief that one can become a werewolf or wolf

mass hysteria–a very strong fear that is held by many people at the same time

mythology–old stories of the gods, people, and early times of the world

nomadic–moving from one place to another; not living for long in one area

persecution–making someone suffer because of who the person is or what he or she believes

predestined–set or fated before it happens

prejudice–belief that one knows in advance the honesty, goodness, and abilities of a person, group, or race

radio collar–collar with a radio transmitter that lets a scientist find and follow the animal wearing it at any time

superstition–belief in magic, luck, or legends

territory–area in which a wolf pack lives and hunts

vicious–mean, cruel, violent

wolfsbane–a plant believed able to scare away werewolves

To Learn More

About werewolf movies:

Cohen, Daniel. *Masters of Horror.* New York: Clarion Books, 1984.

Green, Carl R., and William R. Sanford. *Werewolf of London.* Mankato, MN: Crestwood House, 1985.

Powers, Tom. *Movie Monsters.* Minneapolis: Lerner Publications, 1989.

About werewolves and werewolf legends:

Aylesworth, Thomas G. *Werewolves and Other Monsters.* Reading, MA: Addison-Wesley, 1971.

About wolves:

Johnson, Sylvia A., and Alice Aamodt. *Wolf Pack: Tracking Wolves in the Wild.* Minneapolis: Lerner Publications, 1985.

Lawrence, R. D. *Wolves.* San Francisco: Sierra Club Books, 1990.

Mech, L. David. *The Way of the Wolf.* Stillwater, MN: Voyageur Press, 1991.

Photo Credits:
Hollywood Book and Poster: cover, pp. 4, 9, 10-11, 14, 16, 20, 22, 24; The Newberry Library: pp. 27, 28; Layne Kennedy: pp. 32, 34-35, 37, 38, 40, 41.

Index